Reconsider. Refocus. Remember.

Belongs to:

____

A GUIDED JOURNAL

Believe

A few years ago, as I was praying, the Lord showed me that I was living as a Christian, but not as a *believer*. Having met the Lord at the age of five and serving Him for many years through multiple ministries and short-term mission experiences, this was a convicting revelation from the Holy Spirit.

I was in year ten or so of what I call "my cave." A period where all the visions and plans I thought God had given me were confronted with radically different circumstances that seemed to contradict what I had understood as His purposes for my life. This was impacting many areas of my life, particularly as it related to believing God. It also affected the way I approached Him in prayer. My attitude was almost like I was begging for mercy or anything good He could spare for me, instead of seeing prayer as an honest conversation with my loving, heavenly Father, where I was willing to accept His will as the best for me.

I realized I needed to *reconsider* what I was letting my heart believe, *refocus* on the truths of His Word, and *remember* all the ways the Lord had showed himself powerful and faithful throughout my life.

This has been a years-long journey. Shortly after that realization, things in my life went further into a valley that made even less sense! Often times, I felt like I was inside a maze where my futile attempts to understand what was happening just led me down dead-end corridors and I couldn't find a way out. I kept revisiting David's story and reminding myself how his life twisted and turned for years after being annointed as king over Israel, and the moment he was finally crowned.

I thought of Joseph, as he waited 13 years for an answer to his "Why?"

after being sold into slavery by his brothers, and that one, life-changing day when things fell into place, in a way that only God could have orchestrated.

Reading these stories in the Bible, listening to sermons, praying, being prayed for, and the presence of the Holy Spirit, kept me going on days when my belief and hope seemed to fade and waver.

At the beginning of 2020, the verse I felt the Lord wanted me to keep front and center, was Luke 1:45,

> "Blessed is she who has believed that the Lord would fulfill his promises to her."

Little did I know what the year had in store, including a pandemic that has deeply impacted our world, on top of all the individual things we were each facing at that time. The decision to believe God still has purposes and plans, that He is faithful, that He will never leave us, that He is for us, and that His ways are perfect and higher than ours is essential for persevering.

In the middle of all this, the Lord has ministered to me things that I believe have the power to see me through these challenging times and allow me to live, not just as a Christian who prays, goes to church, listens to Christian music, and does the typical "Christian things," but as a *believer* who takes God at His word, **always**. A person who lives as though she truly belives everything God has said is true and dependable.

Part of those truths deal with how God sees unbelief and how we can deal with it in our lives. This short book presents questions that encourage us to reconsider, refocus, and remember, which are practices that can help stir up our faith to grow and endure when we face valleys, instead of allowing them to distance us from our Savior. It doesn't mean that we will understand everything, but these questions can help us view things through a Biblical lens, instead of through our distorted lens of limited reasoning and perspective.

Believing in God vs. Believing God

Accepting Jesus' sacrifice and the message of the Gospel is one thing, but trusting God in your daily walk and taking Him at his word is another. We can choose to adopt Biblical principles in our lives easily, but maybe struggle believing Him for specific details in our lives. In areas like relationships, health, dreams/goals, and finances, amongst others.

Believing God is not believing that He will answer all I am praying for. It's believing that when He **does not** answer as I would like, His love, sovereignty, Word, and attributes continue being real and that what He does, or allows to be done to us, can work together for our good (Rom.8:28). That He is powerful enough to keep the world spinning and personal enough to hear even my sighs.

How Do We Reflect We Are Not Believing God?

This unbelief, be it hidden or expressed, can permeate and alter areas of our life if it goes unaddressed. How I live, my reactions to situations and problems, and my decisions are all an external expression of what I believe **about** God and whether or not I believe **Him**.

If I know Scripture says that obedience is more important to Him than sacrifice (1 Sam.15:22), yet I choose to continue living in sin in any area of my life, I am showing that, in essence, I don't believe God's word is true, that His commands are for my well-being and that I will, in fact, reap what I sow.

I can go to church as much as I want, but if that does not affect my decision-making and my obedience, I demonstrate that deep down, I **don't believe** God is a jealous God, or that He knows what is best for me, and that I have not decided to follow Him come what may.

In my life, when I find myself in the pit of "this will never change," my unbelief comes floating right up! It shows me that I am not believing God is a good Father, because I am expecting nothing from Him, almost like He would abruptly decide, "I've had enough of her. She can go figure life out for herself." Something that I, as a flawed, imperfect mother can't imagine feeling towards my own children, yet somehow think God, who is *LOVE*, could feel towards me?

When someone does me wrong and I succumb to fear, am I forgetting that "No weapon forged against me will prosper" (Is.54:17)? Am I truly believing His word for my life? If I am honest, I am not. And therein lies my struggle. I need to not only read Scripture, but internalize it and make it part of my constant thinking. This is why Paul said we must be "transformed by the renewing of your mind. Then you will be able to test and approve what God's will is–His good, pleasing and perfect will" (Rom.12:2).

All this begets the question: How can I believe that which is unknown? If I don't know what God says in Scripture, how can that shape my belief? If I don't know what His promises are, how can I pray them over my life? The truth is, I must first **know** His words to then **apply** them in order to live a life that is not marked by despair, unbelief, and defeat.

Where else can we find that? Whose words have power to transform us so? No one's! Only His words are living and powerful, and that should be reason enough for me to desire them. Yet, my human nature tends towards laziness, towards relying only on what I hear in a sermon at church on Sunday, or the verse of the day in an app. But to experience the transforming power of His words in our lives, we must spend time reading His word and memorizing Scripture. This also fuels our belief in Him. Not knowing His words is one of the main reasons we doubt, but certainly not the only one.

Why Do We Doubt?

Past Disappointments

All of us have experienced the disappointment of being let down by someone who told us they would do X or Y, only to leave us waiting and frustrated when they didn't. So, when we think about the reasons we doubt, it's easy to put previous disappointments at the top of the list.

This also applies to our relationship with God. We remember a prayer for healing that wasn't answered as we hoped, or that resulted in the death of a loved one. A marriage that was not restored, while another marriage with worse problems was restored. Genuine, faith-filled requests that seemed to get stuck in the waiting line in heaven.

And slowly, we start doubting God really listens to us and our prayers. That with everything He has going on in the world, my desperate prayer for a new job is ignored. After all, at least I have a job, even if I don't like it. And we grow cold, distant, doubtful; resigned to a "whatever will be, will be" mindset, and hoping to make it through another day, not fully experiencing the joy of the Lord or His rivers of living water.

We imagine God shares character traits of people that have let us down, and quickly lose sight of His goodness and providence. We don't fully internalize that God is interested in us and that He loves us as a perfect Father. Our theology can get foggy if we don't have His truth to fight against our limited, rational thinking, and our natural tendency to protect ourselves from getting hurt emotionally by trusting too much. ·

As children, we were gullible and prone to believe whatever we were told. As we grow older, we develop a sense of distrust in others to avoid getting hurt. I think this is something necessary and normal that God gives us for our protection, but sometimes we come to the Lord with that same wall of distrust. However, what Scripture reveals to us is His constant, ardent desire to be loved and trusted by His children, fully and wholeheartedly.

This takes priority over what we can *do for* Him, or even what we *have done* through ministry. We could be deceived into thinking that if we serve God, then He should spare us from bad things happening in life. But that is not what the Scriptures reveal.

On the contrary, we know that Jesus himself was not exempt from pain and suffering. We live in an imperfect world, which implies that we will experience imperfection and suffering. Jesus warned us about this and we can learn from His life and the lives of men and women who served God through thick and thin (see John 16:33 and Heb. 2, 4, and 11).

God never said we would not encounter affliction. In fact, Jesus was "a man of suffering, and familiar with pain" (Is.53). Therefore, He can understand our pain and lives to intercede for us (Heb.7:25). What God **does** promise is to be with us in our brokenness and that nothing will separate us from His love (Rom.8:31-39). It is heartbreaking when we let hardships separate us from the One who bore the weight of our sin, simply because we are not able to understand why He allows certain things to happen.

It is natural to experience sadness and even deep depression. Many people in Scripture went through both. Jesus himself said, "My soul is overwhelmed with sorrow to the point of death" and on the cross He cried out, "My God, my God, why have you forsaken me?" (Mk. 14:34, Mt.27:46). But remember that Gethsemane and the cross were followed by His resurrection and triumph over death.

If this is where you find yourself, allow God to speak to your heart through these pages. Ask Him to help you overcome your trial and that you can fix your eyes on His goodness and purposes. God is not done with you. This is His story and He's not finished yet.

We Forget

Another reason we doubt is simply because we forget. Often, I feel like my short-term memory with the Lord is embarassing to say the least. I can go from praise to desperation in a matter of minutes. The Lord has proven Himself faithful in my life over and over, yet as deadlines loom, as I wait for a diagnosis, as unwanted loneliness becomes part of my life, as anxiety and tensions mount and the waiting periods stretch, my knees shake, my eyes become water fountains, and the world becomes a scary place about to swallow me up. Jesus tells me to not be afraid, that He has overcome the world, but what I nurture are thoughts that the world is certainly overcoming me.

Because the Lord knows this about us, He constantly urges us through Scripture to remember. In Psalm 78, the first few verses talk about the importance of sharing stories of deliverance and provision from the Lord with our children and future generations:

> "...we will tell the next generation the
> praiseworthy deeds of the Lord, His
> power and the wonders he has done.
> He decreed statutes for Jacob
> and established the law in Israel, which
> he commanded our ancestors
> to teach their children, so the next
> generation would know them, even the
> children yet to be born, and they in
> turn would tell their children. Then
> they would put their trust in God
> and would not forget his deeds
> but would keep his commands." v.4-7

In Joshua 4, when the Lord split the waters of the Jordan river so the Israelites could cross on dry land, the Lord told Joshua to have twelve men, one from each tribe, gather 12 stones from the river and set them up in the middle of their camp. These stones were to be a memorial to the people of Israel forever, to remind them how God had split the waters of the river for them to walk through.

This was not the first time God had split waters. With Moses, it had been the Red Sea (Ex.14), which was far bigger than the Jordan River, and they essentially forgot all about that! This time, God wanted to make sure they would have a visible reminder of these things, because He knew about our short-term memory problem.

One thing I need to add to my life are reminders, memorials if you will, about miracles and ways God has taken care of me and my children. I do that primarily with a yearly photo book I print for my girls. I add notes on how God blessed us and add any memorabilia to go along with it. I also share with them testimonies of friends for which I have been praying, especially very specific prayers which seemed impossible, but that He answered.

One such case was a dear friend who was estranged from her children for over nine years. She had two grandkids she had never met and her pain was unbearable. We prayed and fasted, and things were moving, but at a very slow pace.

I remember praying specifically, "Lord, please, have something happen before the end of the year." A few weeks later, her father passed away, and in an incredible turn of events, all three of her children showed up at the funeral. So, she was able to see them and talk to them a little bit then. It was a bittersweet moment for her, but one that God used to give her hope.

Still, another year went by after that and she had not been able to reconnect with her children despite her many efforts. As I fasted and prayed for her, I felt a desperation in my spirit and prayed, "Lord, this is too much! I pray she's hugging those grandchildren before this year is over."

That was in December, and to be frank, my mind was telling me, "If she's never even met them and they literally live on the other side of the country, how is that even possible?" But that was my prayer.

A few days before Christmas, I got a call from my friend. "My daughter texted me. She wants me to come visit them for Christmas. I'm leaving next Tuesday." Of course, I started to cry and praise the Lord. Talk about an answer to prayer! She was hugging and kissing those babies before the year was over and they are now a part of her life.

Has all been restored? No. But this is an encouraging memory she can look to when doubts start whispering that full restoration with her other children will never come.

And her testimony is not just for her, but for my own faith as I continue praying for things that have already been uttered hundreds of times. This experience was the result of years of prayers by my friend and the brothers and sisters who interceded on her behalf.

I also share stories with my children, about my life and God's provision, through a rememberance journal. This is something I want to keep working on, and one of the reasons I created this guided journal: to have an easy, accesible place to write thoughts and experiences to help me remember God's faithfulness when I face other trials.

How Does God View Unbelief?

In Scripture, there are many examples of people that faced unbelief, hopelessness, and physical and spiritual exhaustion. But from what I have studied, I see two ways that God reacts to unbelief:

> a- It provokes Him to anger *or*
> b- He responds with mercy

Provoked to Anger

In Psalm 78, we see a very clear example of how Israel's unbelief, despite constantly seeing the miraculous deliverance from the Lord, provoked His anger, resulting in the deaths of thousands.

As we read this powerful psalm, we can feel the sense of desperation in the voice of Asaph, the writer. He's like, "You guys, He split the sea and the water stood firm like a wall. He fed them the bread of angels! He made water come out of a rock...a **rock**! He rained meat on them!" But because of their unbelief:

> "They spoke against God; they said, "Can God
> really spread a table in the wilderness?
> True, he struck the rock, and water gushed out,
> streams flowed abundantly, but can he also
> give us bread? Can he supply meat for

> his people?" When the Lord heard
> them, he was furious; his fire broke out
> against Jacob, and his wrath rose against
> Israel, for they did not believe in God or
> trust in his deliverance... In spite of all this,
> they kept on sinning; in spite of his wonders,
> they did not believe." Ps. 78: 19-22, 32

When I read that passage, I tremble. I pray that the attitude of my heart is not of defiant rebellion against God, but that when my humanity and forgetfulness affect my ability to trust in Him, I come with a humble heart, like the one shown by the father of the demon-possesed boy Jesus delivered, "I do believe; help me overcome my unbelief!" (Mark 9:24).

And that is the main difference, the attitude of our heart. Look at verses 36-39 of Psalm 78:

> "But then they would flatter him with
> their mouths, lying to him with their tongues;
> their hearts were not loyal to him, they
> were not faithful to his covenant. Yet he was
> merciful; he forgave their iniquities and
> did not destroy them. Time after time he
> restrained his anger and did not stir up
> his full wrath. He remembered that they were
> but flesh, a passing breeze that does not return."

The Israelites had witnessed what no other nation had: the presence of the living God dwelling with mere mortals. He had done so many wonderful miracles to deliver them from slavery, and all had been eye-witnesses to these wonders. To top it off, He wanted to dwell within His people, and even spoke to them audibly. But they could not handle it, so they asked Moses to be the one to speak with Him.

To make matters worse, their short-term memory was terrible. They murmured against the Lord and even longed to go back to Egypt for some garlic and onions (Nm.11:5)!

But over and over, the Lord provided for all they were craving and demanding. When Moses spent 40 days with God receiving His commandments, they went as far as creating a golden calf and praising it, thanking **the calf** for bringing them out of Egypt.

This provoked God to anger because He had displayed His power to them more than any people had ever seen and yet, they still doubted and rebelled against Him in their hearts. And it brought consequences for the people.

Consequences like the sudden death of many Israelites (Nm.11:33) and, for that generation, the wandering around in the desert for 40 years, not being able to enter the promised land, precisely because they doubted they could take possession of Canaan. They believed the word of ten incredulous spies over the words and acts of God and the encouragement of two spies that did believe (Nm.13, 14).

Having a defiant attitude, like the Israelites, "Can God really set a table in the desert?," will limit me from seeing clearly what God is doing and has done for me. Instead of having a heart of gratitude and trust, I can fall into anxiety, despair, and anger against God.

Another example of defiant unbelief gone terribly bad, is found in 2 Kings 7. I encourage you to read this story and look for similar instances in the Bible that teach us how unbelief impacts our lives. If you don't know how to study the Bible, a good idea is to find a brother or sister in Christ who can teach you.

There are also many online resources that can be beneficial. A ministry that I really like and who's resources I use frequently is *BibleProject*. They have a website and YouTube channel where they offer free videos on the books of the Bible, as well as specific topics, including how to study the Bible.

This is an extensive topic with many Bible passages we could reference. I include only a few in order to maintain brevity and move on to the journaling portion. As you will find, not all unbelief moved God to anger, some moved Him to mercy.

Moved to Mercy

I have already mentioned the father of the demon-possessed boy and how Jesus responded to his honest confession of belief mixed with doubt. And likewise, there are many other stories like that one in Scripture. We see it when Peter stepped out of the boat to walk on water towards Jesus, but started sinking as the doubts crept in. Jesus didn't just let him drown to set an example for the other disciples! He lifted him up and asked "Why did you doubt?" (Mt.14:31).

On other occasions, the rest of the disciples doubted too. Even though they had seen the multiplication of bread and fish, when they encountered another hungry crowd, they doubted again! Twice Jesus multiplied food for crowds, and twice they doubted.

Jesus takes note of those who believe without seeing, "...Blessed are those who have not seen and yet have believed" (John 20:29). He knows that seeing miracles and wonders does not guarantee belief. We must **choose** to believe. Confessing our lack of belief, but declaring our decision to believe is an act of faith that moves our gracious God to mercy.

Another example is the widow of Zarephath (1 Kings 17). God chose a woman who had no one to sustain her, to supply for the prophet in that particular moment during a famine. At the beginning of the story, when Elijah finds her, she had already lost all hope of surviving. She was gathering sticks to cook one last meal for her and her son and then "die." Elijah asked her to give him food first and she believed his words and did what he asked. That small act of faith moved God's hand in her favor. The little bit of flour and oil she had did not run out for the duration of the famine.

After the famine, her son died, which led the woman to doubt and complain against the prophet. She had been witnessing a daily miracle for three years, which might make us think her faith would increase every time she reached into the jars and kept finding flour and oil.

But as her circumstances changed drastically and she faced an even more impossible situation, the death of her son, she doubted. Her humanity and suffering made her doubt and react with desperation.

Yet, she found grace once again. Her action of coming to God and the prophet moved the Lord to mercy, and He raised her son back to life! And then she concluded, "Now I know that you are a man of God and that the word of the Lord from your mouth is the truth." Lesson learned.

As we walk with Jesus and desire to grow in our faith, we will go through experiences like these. God answers a prayer and we are ready to conquer the world. But when hard times come and we don't see a tangible answer from Him, will we still believe He is sovereign and in control? Or will we shake our fist up in the air and yearn for Egypt? As our faith matures, we need to learn not to let circumstances dictate our belief in what God has said, but to trust regardless of our doubts and brokenness.

What Can We Do?

When trials and uncertainties come, there are several things we can do to help keep our focus on Jesus and not on what we don't understand. We can:

- Choose to believe (Heb.11:6)
- Remember what He has done before (1 Chr.16:8-12)
- Read, internalize, and listen to Scripture (Rom.10:17)
- Praise God and study His promises for our lives and remember specific words He has spoken over us (Ps. 103)
- Fast, pray, and ask our brothers and sisters to pray for us, especially when we are too exhausted to even pray

These are some of the ways God has provided for us to build up our faith and hope in His words.

One of my favorite prayers in the Bible came from an impossibly hopeless situation King Jehoshaphat and the Israelites encountered. There were several kings that joined forces to fight against them. They were greatly outnumbered and the logical outcome was certain death for all of them. Period. However, Jehoshaphat proclaimed a fast for all Judah and they sought the Lord.

As he finished his prayer, he said, "...we have no power to face this vast army that is attacking us. We do not know what to do, but our eyes are on you" (2 Chr.20:12).

My friend, I have been there so many times. With hardships surrounding me and not sure of what do. But when it's hard to sing "You are never going to let me down...," when I lift my eyes to the heavens, I experience the loving mercy of my Father, and enough grace to see me through another day.

And that grace is available to you too. That call from the Lord to grow in intimacy with Him in the middle of your valley is an opportunity. An opportunity to grow in faith and to experience the salvation and provision that only He can provide.

As Jehoshaphat and the people prayed, the Spirit of the Lord came upon a Levite, Jahaziel, and the Lord spoke through him saying,

"Do not be afraid or discouraged
because of this vast army. For the
battle is not yours, but God's... You will
not have to fight this battle. Take up
your positions; stand firm and see
the deliverance the Lord will give you,
Judah and Jerusalem. Do not be
afraid, do not be discouraged. Go out
to face them tomorrow, and
the Lord will be with you."
2 Chr.20:15b, 17

The next morning, they marched, singing and praising the Lord for the splendor of His holiness. As they sang, the Lord set ambushes against their enemies and they destroyed one another. When the men of Judah arrived, all the soldiers from the enemy's armies were dead! Not only did they not have to fight the battle, but the plunder they took was so much, it took them three days to collect it. All because they chose to believe God's plan, God's words to them, and walk onward with praise.

I can imagine that was not easy. A lot of them might have been thinking, "Our plan is to face this army singing? What kind of plan is that?" They probably thought they would be mocked for their "strategy." But nonetheless, they chose to believe God's words and keep going with their *concert*. Because of that decision, they saw God's glory and power, and in the end, called that place the Valley of Berakah, or blessing.

In our valleys, God gives us a wonderful weapon: worship. It may seem simple, but truly all He asks us is to worship as we walk, believing Him. He wants us to trust Him. No matter how many armies come against us. He will fight for us. He will turn our valley into a place of blessing.

Why I Wrote This Journal

In 2016, I experienced the worst crisis of my life. What I valued most in life was crumbling right in front of me, and none of the things I tried to stop it worked. I fasted, prayed, sought counseling, heard messages, everything. But heaven seemed shut to my cries for help.

I faced so many questions and uncertainties that many days I couldn't even think straight. My thoughts were on a never-ending loop. For weeks, all I could pray was, "Send your light and your truth and they will guide me," yearning, hoping to hear from my Lord (see Ps.43:3 CSB).

And He did speak to me, in so many ways I could write a book just about the this season of my life. But one particular day, as I was driving to church, I felt He sent a ray of light and truth over me, right there in my car. I began preaching out loud to myself. Scripture after Scripture flowing by His Spirit and strengthening my soul. Moved by His presence, I thanked Him, and with conviction said, "This is it, Lord. This is where my unbelief ends. From now on, I am going to believe you. I don't know why you have allowed all this pain, but I am going to trust in your sovereignty."

I felt hopeful that day, but I quickly realized this was not a once in a lifetime decision. This had to be my decision every day in the years that followed. The days when I felt his light and truth flooding my car, and the days when I felt myself drowning in a flood of despair. Those days when I felt numb and almost sure my eyes had run out of tears. The days when nothing made sense, and the days I felt I could tackle the book of Revelation! I have to *choose* to believe. **Every. Single. Day.**

As I faced this process, I realized that I was going to have to fight the battle in my mind with strategy, or I would not survive. This process, as often occurs with "caves," "prisons," and moments of preparation from the Lord, was also a very lonely time. There are pains and experiences that just can't be shared.

In those months, I began longing for questions that would help me order my thoughts so that I could point out the enemy's lies and what I needed to do to help my unbelief. And that's where the idea for this journal came up.

I wrote it praying and hoping it can help others going through difficult times to find truth and light to see them through to the other side. Light and truth that can awaken our hearts to worship that transforms our valleys.

I have developed a deeper sense of compassion for those who suffer and I wish I could sit down and have a cup of coffee with you to listen to your story and encourage you through your trial.

But since that is not possible, I offer you these thoughts, questions, and encouragement so that you too can reconsider, refocus, and remember the Lord's power and mercies, and trust Him with your battles in the face of unbelief.

How To Use This Journal

The purpose of making this a short book and journal is so it can be reused for subsequent trials or valleys. You can order new copies for different situations, or simply use a separate notebook to copy and answer the questions again.

I have divided the journal into three parts:

- Reconsider
- Refocus
- Remember

You can answer the questions in whichever order you prefer. This is your place to process what you are going through. A place to take notes and search in Scripture for truths that apply to your situation and write those verses down. I share verses that have meant a lot to me in these years, as well as prayers, poems, songs, and photos I have taken. Some pages are left blank intentionally. These are for you to get creative! You can add scribbles, drawings, stickers, verses, anything that can help you refocus your situation.

These are some other ways I rest in God: I hike, travel, go on nature walks to take photos, visit national parks, and go outside to breathe fresh air when I feel I can't go on. Brokenness often helps us notice things that would otherwise go unseen. I find healing in the Lord's creation. I find glimpses of a caring, masterful Designer who creates beautiful things for His praise and my enjoyment, and that gives me faith, as I remember that is the God I serve and the God who is for me.

It reminds me that He cares about me, and that He will not fail. He calls me His masterpiece, and loved me so much He came to the world to be broken for me.

He loves you, my friend. He is "close to the brokenhearted and saves those who are crushed in spirit" (Ps.34:18). Your situation and your pain are real and God understands how you feel. Come as you are. Draw near to Him in your valleys. Pour out your heart, tears, and complaints in His presence. Keep seeking His face, keep asking for His light and His truth and He will pour them over you. He will shelter you. He will fight for you.

Write a prayer asking the Lord to guide you through this journal:

Believe

"But now, this is what the Lord
says—he who created you, Jacob,
he who formed you, Israel;
"Do not fear, for I have redeemed
you; I have summoned you by
name; you are mine.
When you pass through the waters,
I will be with you;
and when you pass through the rivers,
they will not sweep over you.
When you walk through fire,
you will not be burned;
the flames will not set you ablaze.
For I am the Lord your God,
the Holy One of Israel,
your Savior..."

Is.43:1-3a

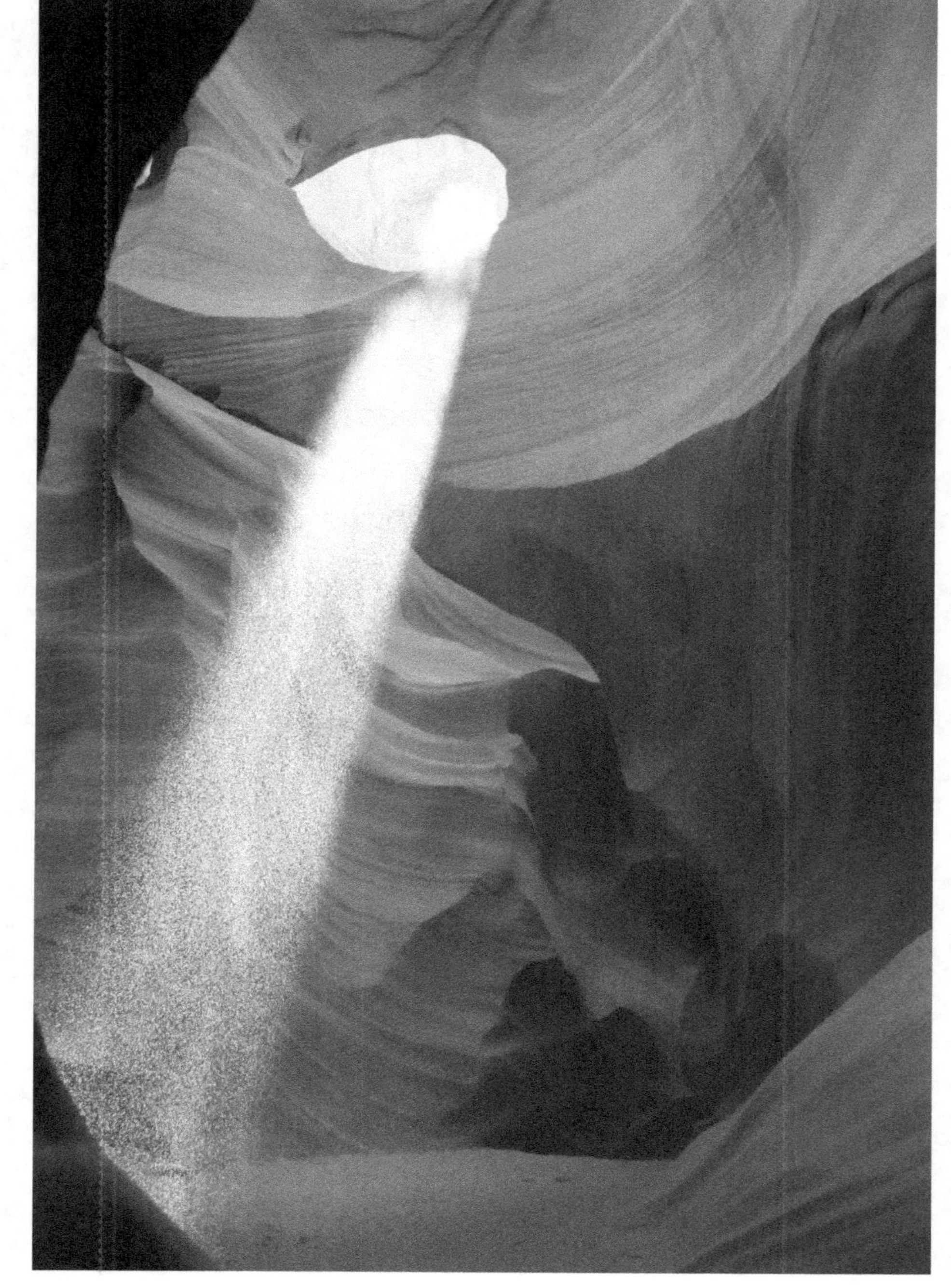

Reconsider

"Send your light and your truth;
let them lead me. Let them bring
me to your holy mountain,
to your dwelling place."

Ps.43:3

Describe your situation

Date: ______________________________

How does this make you feel?

How has this situation affected your life?

What changes have you noticed in you?

Reconsider

What does God think about this?

How do you know?

What verses reveal God's point of view on the subject?

Has this situation changed your perception of God?

Who Are You Listening To?

As you walk through your trial, it is important to consider who you listen to and who you share your situation and questions with. During my process, I was able to take a trip by myself to seek the Lord and rest after a period of working full-time and also homeschooling.

The first day of the trip, after a beautiful day with the Lord in the wilderness, I came back to civilization and to phone service. I found I had a text message from a well-intentioned friend, but whose words hurt me deeply. She only knew a few bits and pieces of my situation, but she sent me a message detailing what I needed to do and what God was **NEVER** going to do, unless I took such and such steps (yes, she wrote it in all caps).

It was devastating because I felt completely misunderstood and judged. But as soon as I read the text, the Holy Spirit put scriptures in my mind that showed me why what she was saying was wrong and did not come from Him. However, the damage had been done. I cried over that text message all week long.

When I came home, as I was getting ready for church, and still thinking about the text, the Lord spoke these words very clearly to my heart: "Don't give her words more power than my words." I was confronted with how much time and energy I had spent having imaginary conversations with this person, trying to explain why her statement was Biblically inaccurate and also hurtful. I thought to myself, when was the last time I gave as much thought to God's words about me? How often did one of His promises keep me up at night?

I decided that, even though I care deeply for this friend, she was not someone who I would confide in or share the struggles of this particular valley.

Instead, the Lord brought older women into my life to speak words of wisdom and truth in love, based on their own experiences with brokenness and their walk with Jesus.

Sometimes, pain will cause your closest friends to distance themselves, maybe too overwhelmed with your situation. But even though that can happen, God will bring to your life the people that are going to help you heal and lift you up. So, choose carefully who you share your heart with, and what you share.

Write a prayer for wisdom in choosing friends:

Write the names of wise friends and relatives you can reach out to for advice and support:

Have your circumstances changed your perception of life?

Have they changed your perception of others? How so?

What do you think this situation says about you?

Are those thoughts aligned with Scripture?

Reconsider

What lies is the enemy trying to make you believe? Be specific and use Biblical truths to refute them (see Matthew 4:1-11).

Lie:

Truth:

Lie:

Truth:

Lie:

Truth:

Lie:

Truth:

Lie:

Truth:

Lie:

Truth:

Lie:

Truth:

Lie:

Truth:

Lie:

Truth:

Lie:

Truth:

Lie:

Truth:

"Lord, you do not withhold your compassion from me. Your constant love and truth will always guard me." Ps.40:11

What do you fear? How does God address those fears in Scripture?

Fear:

Truth:

Fear:

Truth:

Fear:

Truth:

Fear:

Truth:

Fear:

Truth:

"The Lord is with me; I will not be afraid. What can mere mortals do to me?" Ps.118:6

What expectations did you have?

What disappointments do you need to let go of?

Reconsider

Are there other things you need to let go, like friendships, memorabilia that provokes sadness (photos/objects/songs/places), grudges, etc.?

Are you focused on the past? What can you learn from Isaiah 43:15-19?

Look up verses that deal with worry and write one or two below:

Reconsider

If you are dealing with a difficult person, what boundaries can you establish to guard your heart?

"Above all else, guard your heart, for everything you do flows from it." Pr.4:23

Read Galatians 5. What acts of the flesh do you see in your life? What fruit of the Spirit?

What comes to mind when you think of **contentment**?

Read Philipians 4:4–13

Would you say your satisfaction is coming from Jesus?

Don't (A Song for My Soul)

Don't let yourself go
Don't lose your will and your hope
Don't waste the rest of your life
'Cause somebody said, "You won't..."

Don't let fear be your guide
Don't quench the fire that's inside
Don't let doubt conquer your faith
When all that He says is "Believe"

Oh my soul, oh my soul...believe

Look at what is unseen
Drink from His living streams
Sing a song that breaks through the night
Darkness will know you believe

Oh my soul, oh my soul...believe

You will shine, you will reach
all that you're meant to be
You will soar, you will live
by His strength and His love
You're not alone, He'll never leave
or forsake what He owns
Oh my soul, oh my soul...believe

Oh my soul, don't give in...
Don't let yourself go

Reconsider

Do you need to surrender your life or something else to Jesus? Write
your prayer:

How is your faith growing in this process?

What attitudes do you need to work on?

Additional notes:

Reconsider

Perspective

When I was in high school, God surprised me with a student trip I won during my senior year. I went to Mexico and it was a lovely time in my life and a testimony of the kindness God bestows upon His children. Looking out the window as we flew over Mexico, I saw two things that moved me deeply. We were flying over a carpet of white clouds that covered the entire panorama. On the horizon, the peak of an imposing volcano broke through the cloud barrier. I was so impressed, I literally cried. It was the first time I saw a view like that one and the size of the mountain blew my mind.

The second thing was a lesson God taught me visually. I believe He did so because He knew that, as an artist, I would understand the lesson better if I saw it. As we prepared to land, I looked out the window and saw the cars driving below us like tiny ants parading in line through a forest floor.

I noticed that from the plane I had a privileged view, or perspective, above that of the drivers below. I could see all the intersections and could anticipate cars' movements before they happened. Furthermore, from this view point I could easily foresee an accident. God ministered to me that, in the same way, He has a privileged perspective over my life. I see the traffic light that stops me, or the pedestrian that crosses suddenly in front of my car, forcing me to drive cautiously. But I can't see the truck headed my way two blocks down the road, maybe without brakes or driving erratically.

God can see these things because His perspective is much higher than mine, perfect in fact. It's complete, because He is not limited by time: He sees the past, the present, and the future.

When I focus only on my problem, it's as if I was stuck in a traffic jam, complaining about it, when it might well be the tool God is using to save my life. One day, after ending my work shift, I took an alternate route home. To my surprise, there was a road block along this alternate road and I got pulled over for having an expired tag on my car. They gave me a $200 ticket. Obviously, I was not happy about the ticket, but had a sense of peace because I thought that maybe if I had taken the usual road, I would have had a fatal accident or something. If God allowed the fine, knowing it was a huge amount for me, then I trusted He knew what He was delivering me from on the other road.

It was an enlightening moment for me. And, at my young age, I thought I would never forget that illustration, which would remind me of God's sovereignty and prevision during trials, thus allowing me to trust in Him blindly. The truth is, I didn't forget the lesson. But the other truth is that when the problems and trials of life are more difficult than those I had when I was 17 years old, it's not as easy to believe that God's providence is sparing me from suffering something worse down the road. When things are upside down, how do you believe it's all part of God's plan? The *original* plan, not an emergency one because something escaped His attention and now He's scrambling for a solution.

How I struggle with this lesson! It's so easy to listen to another believer's story and tell them, "Don't worry, God's in control. He knows what He's delivering you from, everything will be ok, you'll see."

However, believing that over our own lives and circumstances can be very hard! Sometimes, we need to take a step back and try to see things from a different perspective.

Sometimes, when God speaks to us and shares what He wants to do, or where He wants us to go, we think we are going there right away.

However, from what I see in Scripture, and my own life and those of other believers, God rarely takes us from point A to point B and BOOM!, you have arrived. He'll take us from A to G, to C, to T, and so on. If we compare it to a board game, God's ways are frequently like *Chutes and Ladders*. We take a step and go up a ladder, three steps later, we're down a chute. We move again and climb up a ladder, then we take a detour and end up where we started! I'm talking about the route, not our well-being.

Consider Paul, for example. He didn't turn into the Paul we know over night. God gave him a huge calling when He initially revealed Himself to him, but Paul didn't write his letters the day after he recovered his eyesight! It took YEARS of processes and lessons. In fact, in his letter to the Romans, we can see that even though he was already recognized in his ministry, he too desired to be encouraged mutually in his faith with other believers (Rom.1:12).

If Paul hadn't spent so much time in jail, he might not have felt the urgency to write to believers. Did he have any idea the entire world would be able to read those letters? I doubt it. Instead, he could have become bitter inside a smelly prison, but he decided to use his prisons to share truths that God has used for thousands of years.

From Paul's perspective, he might have seen a small group of believers reading and sharing his letters. On the other hand, God knew that those letters would teach us about Christian living, that they would inspire thousands and thousands of books, sermons, conversations, dissensions, and even a journal like this one.

Why does God work in this way in our lives? One reason is because He is in the process of maturing us and growing us to the measure of the fullness of Christ. "Consider it a great joy, my brothers and sisters, whenever you experience various trials, because you know that the testing of your faith produces endurance. And let endurance have its full effect, so that you may be mature and complete, lacking nothing" (James 1:2-4, see also Eph.4:13).

Oh, but how we want to understand everything at once! "Lord, why are you allowing me to go through this? Why didn't you heal him? Why did you take this person from my life? Why didn't they give me the opportunity? Why can't I have the family I desire?" And so many other questions we ask Jesus. Questions that don't necessarily have answers that will satisfy our limited minds, which only when we see Him face to face we might understand.

I say *might* because I don't think that when I finally see Him in all His majesty I'm going to be like, "So, hey Lord, why didn't I get that promotion back in 2018?" I think that none of the things that bog us down will have any more importance. Hmm, that sounds like our perspective will be completely different. Could it be that we'll finally understand that He doesn't need our permission to work in the world? That nobody taught Him how to create the Earth, and that He doesn't lack all the details of what is happening to us (which we want to make sure we tell him about)?

Immediately, I think about Job, who went through unimaginable pain and who questioned God eloquently for a mere mortal. The same way that we often do. The same way Mary and Martha did, "Lord, if you had been here, my brother would not have died..." (John 11:21).

You know? Questioning God is not something bad in itself; Scripture is full of examples of God's servants doing so. He knows that from our perspective, we can't see the entire panorama. Talk to Him, tell Him how you feel, but recognize His sovereignty through it all. "Not my will, but yours be done," "Your will be done, on earth as it is in heaven" (Lk.22:42, Mt.6:10).

After Job vented through his questions and speeches, God answered with His own set of questions and observations. I suggest you read all of God's answer to Job, because in it, there are beautiful details about God's creative power.

Let us consider that God could have responded in many different ways: explaining that Satan had asked for permission to tempt Job, rebuking him for being so brazen, staying quiet or ignoring Job's questions, to name a few. However, God responds by making much of His own power and greatness. A lot of His response is based on describing things He created, including a very specific description of the leviathan, which sounds an awful lot like a dragon or some extinct beast for us, but one with which Job was familiar. That's something I do want ask God about in heaven!

Think about God's answer. In essence, what He does is highlight a tiny portion of His resume. Enough to silence Job's complaints. He removes Job and his situation from the focal point, and places the attention on God and His creative power. God and His plans. God and His omniscience. God and His glory.

This is the key that allows us to walk one day at a time when we are crossing a valley. *It's changing our perspective from an egocentric one, obsessed with understanding the reason for the pain, to one that is centered around God's greatness and power.*

Of course, we can't forget all the beautiful promises God has for us, or the restoration God brought to Job's life. But look at Job's attitude after hearing from God: he humbled himself and recognized God's power. When we have the attitude to learn from God, God honors that and takes us from glory to glory.

When we get irritated against God for our suffering, we get stuck, embittered, and stop growing.

Friend, God is not unaware of our pain. He has not forgotten you. He is working even when it seems nothing is happening. Where will we anchor our confidence? In our limited human understanding or in the One who has power to create invincible dragons? On Him who calls each star by its name, who knows how many hairs are on our heads, who creates beasts of the field, who gives life to that which was dead and who creates things where there was nothing?

Reconsider

Maybe you can't board a plane right this minute to literally change your perspective, but maybe a stroll in a nearby forest can help you focus on the things He's created. A bird's song reminds you that if He cares for the birds, He cares for you. A noisy insect reminds you that all creation worships Him. A sunset reminds you that His mercy will be renewed in just a few more hours and that joy comes in the morning.

I close with some of my favorite verses from God's response to Job in chapter 38:

"Where were you when I laid the earth's foundation?

Tell me, if you understand.

Who marked off its dimensions? Surely you know!

Who stretched a measuring line across it?

On what were its footings set,

or who laid its cornerstone—

while the morning stars sang together

and all the angels shouted for joy?

Who shut up the sea behind doors

when it burst forth from the womb,

when I made the clouds its garment

and wrapped it in thick darkness,

when I fixed limits for it

and set its doors and bars in place,

when I said, 'This far you may come and no farther;

here is where your proud waves halt'?

Have you ever given orders to the morning,

or shown the dawn its place,

that it might take the earth by the edges

and shake the wicked out of it?

The earth takes shape like clay under a seal;

its features stand out like those of a garment.

The wicked are denied their light,

and their upraised arm is broken.

Have you journeyed to the springs of the sea

or walked in the recesses of the deep?
Have the gates of death been shown to you?
Have you seen the gates of the deepest darkness?
Have you comprehended the vast expanses of the earth?
Tell me, if you know all this.
What is the way to the abode of light?
And where does darkness reside?
Can you take them to their places?
Do you know the paths to their dwellings?
Surely you know, for you were already born!
You have lived so many years!
Have you entered the storehouses of the snow
or seen the storehouses of the hail,
which I reserve for times of trouble,
for days of war and battle?
What is the way to the place where the
lightning is dispersed, or the place where the
east winds are scattered over the earth?
Who cuts a channel for the torrents of rain,
and a path for the thunderstorm,
to water a land where no one lives,
an uninhabited desert,
to satisfy a desolate wasteland
and make it sprout with grass?
Does the rain have a father?
Who fathers the drops of dew?
From whose womb comes the ice?
Who gives birth to the frost from the heavens
when the waters become hard as stone,
when the surface of the deep is frozen?
Can you bind the chains of the Pleiades?

Can you loosen Orion's belt?
Can you bring forth the constellations in their seasons
or lead out the Bear with its cubs?
Do you know the laws of the heavens?
Can you set up God's dominion over the earth?
Can you raise your voice to the clouds
and cover yourself with a flood of water?
Do you send the lightning bolts on their way?
Do they report to you, 'Here we are'?
Who gives the ibis wisdom
or gives the rooster understanding?
Who has the wisdom to count the clouds?
Who can tip over the water jars of the heavens
when the dust becomes hard
and the clods of earth stick together?"

Refocus

"Therefore I am now going to
allure her; I will lead her into
the wilderness and speak
tenderly to her."

Hos.2:14

Are there specific instructions in Scripture about your situation?

How do they translate into possible solutions for your situation?

If you knew you were dying tomorrow, what would you most regret? Can you do something about that now?

Has God brought someone to your life you can pray for and invest in? If so, who? How can you shift your focus off your situation to help others?

Who do you know that has gone through a similar situation and come out stronger? Can you set up time to talk with them?

Is there someone praying for you? If that is not the case, find a faithful believer who you can ask to keep you in their prayers.

Who are you praying for consistently?

Is there sin in your life that you need to confess?

Are there things you are watching or listening to that hinder your spiritual growth or encourage sin? Be specific and list the things you need to stop doing or allowing to influence your life.

Refocus

What things are out of your control?

What things **can you** control?

Who do you need to forgive? What exactly do you need to forgive them or yourself for?

Do you need to apologize to someone? Why? When and how will you do so?

Save Me a Place

And I wait for you.
In the silence of my bedroom,
each night, I wait for you.
Every sleepless night looks for its ending
in your words, I yearn for you.

And I seek you.
In every star and in the moon
I see your splendor, I seek you.
I want to hear your voice
in my daughters' laughter, I love you.

Save me a corner in your presence,
a glimpse of your altar.
Save me a place at your table,
just a piece of your bread
and wine. Save me a place.

And I draw near to you.
I tremble just to touch the hem
of your cloak, I draw near to you.
In an instant you can
heal my wounds, I humble myself.

And I give in. My will and reasoning
I will no longer enthrone, I give in.
My thoughts are not enough,
I can not understand, I surrender.

Save me a corner in your presence,
a glimpse of your altar.
Save me a place at your table,
just a piece of your bread
and wine. Save me a place.

Just a little bit of you is enough for me.
It's your great majesty that sustains me.

Describe your devotional life. Do you need to dedicate more time to prayer, Scripture reading, or fasting?

Read Psalms 34 and 37, in various versions. How do these verses minister to your heart?

Read Isaiah 58, is there something you should fast from? How can you separate time for praying and seeking the Lord this week?

Read James 5:13-18. If you are sick, have you asked for prayer and been annointed with oil? If not, consider adding this practice to your life.

Are you overcommitted? Do you need to consider simplifying your commitments?

Do you need a break from social media or the news? If so, establish dates and an action plan.

Do you need to consider professional counseling? Does your church offer any assistance?

What are some ways you can set apart 1-2 hours, at least twice a month, to have a mini-retreat? Can you visit a park, beach, go for a drive, or create a place in your closet to focus without distractions? Come up with a plan and write it here and in your planner.

Refocus

Are there any books you can read that would be helpful in these circumstances? List them here:

____

____

____

____

____

____

What lessons or positive things have you learned through this trial?

Lesson: ______________________________________

____

____

Lesson: ______________________________________

____

____

Lesson: ______________________________________

____

____

Lesson: ______________________________________

____

____

Lesson: ______________________________________

____

____

Lesson: ______________________________________

Lesson:

Lesson:

Lesson:

Lesson:

Lesson:

Lesson:

Lesson:

Lesson:

Lesson:

Refocus

Write verses to memorize:

Verse:

Verse:

Verse:

Verse:

Verse:

Verse:

Verse:

Verse:

Verse:

Verse:

Verse:

Verse:

Verse:

Verse:

Verse:

Verse:

Verse:

Verse:

A Wooly Caterpillar Like Me?

Frequently, God uses nature to teach me or show me living examples of lessons I am processing. That's why I love to watch animal and nature documentaries. My favorites are the ones produced by the BBC, in particular the *Planet Earth* and *Frozen Planet* series. Recently, as I watched an episode of *Frozen Planet*, I saw a natural phenomenon that moved me profoundly.

We've all heard analogies between the metamorphic process of butterflies and our own lives. We often compare our difficult stages in life to their transformation, which can resemble our own struggles before turning into "butterflies."

However, I have felt that many times I go through stage after stage and don't transform into a butterfly! Frequently, I think "certainly after this trial the long awaited opportunity or moment for which God has been preparing me all these years in the desert will arrive." But, the trial ends and nothing. And then, another harder trial...and nothing. I say "nothing," but I know that there's always something to learn and that every life lesson shapes us more into Jesus' character, if we allow it to. So, let me explain what I mean with an example from Scripture that is familiar to us all.

When David was just a youth, his job was to watch his father's sheep. During this time, he grew and matured in his knowledge and love for the Lord. An unexpected day, Samuel shows up and anoints him as the next king of Israel. Some time after being anointed, David defeats Goliath and marries king Saul's daughter. It's likely he could have thought that he was closer than ever to his reign, after all, he worked for the king and was his son in law! But, that's not how it happened.

We know Saul tried to kill David and that David spent years fleeing from him, living in caves and wilderness strongholds (or hard to reach places). In fact, between the anointing and the beginning of his reign, it was about 15 years. Time and time again he faced situations that seemed to be drawing him closer to the destiny God had designed for him, just to be disappointed again. We can read about the internal conflict this caused in David in many of the psalms he wrote.

I have never been anointed as the next *queen*, but from an early age, I believed God had a calling over my life. However, every time I have been close to what I thought could be the destiny or plan God has been preparing, something happens and I end up in a "cave" or a valley of loneliness and isolation in which David's psalms are what God often uses to bring hope and comfort to my life.

Like I mentioned at the beginning of the journal, others who went through similar processes were Joseph, Moses, Abraham... The Bible is full of examples like these, because it is precisely in these valleys and caves that God prepares our hearts. And *Frozen Planet*? Bear with me, I'm getting there.

God created an astounding insect: the wooly bear caterpillar. I don't think I have ever felt more identified with any other insect! This caterpillar lives in the arctic tundras, where winter temperatures average -34°C. In spring, the caterpillar eats quickly before the cold weather returns. However, when winter arrives, the caterpillar does not have enough "reserves" to transform into a moth, a relative of butterflies. Since it cannot yet fly, it can't flee the arctic, so it looks for shelter underneath a rock.

As winter moves in, everything freezes up, including the caterpillar. It stops breathing, its heart stops beating, and the blood stops flowing. Essentially, the caterpillar dies. Months later, when spring returns and the ice melts, miraculously, the caterpillar revives! As if nothing had happened, it goes back to its feeding frenzy, seeking to fill up for its transformation. But over and over, year after year, it's not enough, it's not ready yet. According to *Frozen Planet*, it will be 14 years of this process before the caterpillar is finally ready to turn into a moth!

Year after year, all this caterpillar does is eat and prepare for its destiny. When it's finally ready, it weaves a cocoon, inside which its body will be transformed, developing wings and its searching abilities, which are crucial to its survival.

In the caterpillar's case, the purpose after all this process is to find a mate and reproduce. In our case, as believers, our maturing processes also tend to bring forth new life, as we share with others the truth of the Gospel and God's care as He weaves our story, even if it takes us 14 years or more living in a cave or under a rock!

Notice the wonderful symbolism, that the caterpillar looks for refuge under a rock. Scripture teaches us that Jesus is our rock and that we are secure when we build our life upon Him.

> "Be my rock of refuge, to which I can always
> go; give the command to save me, for you
> are my rock and my fortress." Psalm 71:3

He protects us during times of "freezing;" those moments when we feel like the living dead. He revives us, feeds us, and cares for us jealously, knowing exactly when is the perfect time to let us fly.

I was stunned as I watched these dramatic scenes in the documentary, amazed at the incredible design of our Father, who shows us even through insects how much He loves us, and that He cares for us individually and specifically.

When you feel like God has forgotten you, that you are frozen, that nothing makes sense anymore, remember the wooly bear caterpillar. Remember David running for his life, living like a wild animal in the mountains. Remember Moses, caring for loud, dumb sheep in arid lands for 40 years (the same 40 years he would later lead dumb and loud sheep-like people through the desert after delivering them from Egypt).

Remember Abraham waiting for the promised son, year after year, wrinkle after wrinkle, white hair after white hair. Remember Joseph, forgotten by everyone, without his family, and unjustly imprisoned. **Remember.**

Remember God's mercy over your life on other occasions. Remember His provision and His care. Remember the cross. Remember the presence of the Holy Spirit in your life. Remember the answered prayers. Remember the parted sea, the manna from heaven, and the gentle whisper of His presence.

Abraham became the father of nations. David, the most important king in Israel's history and one of Jesus' great-grandfathers! Joseph, the second in command in Egypt, responsible for saving the lives of millions of people when there was a seven-year famine. Moses spoke with God face to face, became the most humble man on earth (Nm.12:3), and was one of the men present during Jesus' transfiguration.

We don't know what our role will be in the story God is writing, but whatever it is, it will be good because God designed it. John the Baptist prepared the way for Jesus' ministry and he ended up beheaded. Still, he fulfilled his destiny, and Jesus said, "Truly I tell you, among those born of women there has not risen anyone greater than John the Baptist; yet whoever is least in the kingdom of heaven is greater than he" (Mt.11:11).

Being in a cave or under a rock is not the end of your story. Have courage, keep feeding and filling up your reserves so that, when God says it's time, you can fly.

Between the fog and the rainy days
Between the sorrow and the joy
Between the emptyness and the abundance
Between the loneliness and the laughter
Between my insufficiency and your fullness
In everything. From one extreme to the other.
From the highest place to deepest, You.
You my strength. You my breath. You my light.
There is no valley too dark,
no fog too dense.
Nothing separates me from your love,
my beloved, Jesus.

Remember

"Give praise to the Lord, proclaim his
name; make known among the nations
what he has done. Sing to him,
sing praise to him; tell of all
his wonderful acts. Glory in his
holy name; let the hearts of those
who seek the Lord rejoice. Look
to the Lord and his strength; seek
his face always. Remember the
wonders he has done, his miracles,
and the judgements he pronounced…"

1 Chr.16:8-12

What specific word(s) has the Lord ministered to you during this trial? Include how and when He spoke to you. If this was through prophecy, does the prophecy align with Scripture?

If the Lord hasn't spoken to you specifically, I encourage you to keep praying and seeking His face. He will speak to you in a clear way when it is His time.

How have you seen God at work in the middle of this trial or in previous moments of your life? Has there ever been a word spoken over you that came to pass? Explain.

Remember

List previous or current experiences where the Lord worked on your
behalf. For example, a job or financial provision in time of need, a person
who helped you during a crisis, etc.

Need: ____ Date: ________________

____

How God answered: ____

____

____

____

____

Need: ____ Date: ________________

____

How God answered: ____

____

____

____

____

Need: ____ Date: ________________

____

How God answered: ____

____

____

____

____

Need: ____ Date: ________________

____

____

How God answered:

Need: Date:

How God answered:

Need: Date:

How God answered:

Need: Date:

How God answered:

"And my God will meet all your needs according
to the riches of his glory in Christ Jesus." Phil.4:19

Remember

Need: _______________________ Date: _______________________

____

How God answered: ____

____

____

____

____

Need: _______________________ Date: _______________________

____

How God answered: ____

____

____

____

____

Need: _______________________ Date: _______________________

____

How God answered: ____

____

____

____

____

Need: _______________________ Date: _______________________

____

How God answered: ____

____

____

____

Need: ___________________________ Date: ___________________________

How God answered: ___________________________

Need: ___________________________ Date: ___________________________

How God answered: ___________________________

Need: ___________________________ Date: ___________________________

How God answered: ___________________________

Need: ___________________________ Date: ___________________________

How God answered: ___________________________

Lapis Lazuli

On March 14, 2016, I made my way to church almost like a robot. I was on the brink of what would later prove to be the hardest period of my life and, even at this point, was already out of strength and hope. I was fighting for my marriage and feared this was a lost battle. I was physically present, but on autopilot, because my brain was in a fog.

In speaking with a friend a few days before, I told her, "I feel like depleted, done...*poof!*" I was tired and brokenhearted. I did not have much faith or expectation that God would speak to me so clearly that morning, or even less that this would set off a chain of events that later exemplified more vividly than I had ever experienced that God's word is living and effective (Heb.4:12 CSB).

My pastor, Louie Giglio, began his message by sharing the title: *From a Colossal Bust to Royal Blue*. As an artist, that caught my attention right away. He talked about Joseph and how setbacks can be setups in life. He said, "This is your turning point" and that "your pain and suffering can be leveraged for the blessing of many people."

I was drawn into the message, but I almost fell off my chair when he talked about the color royal blue, and how it was such a beautiful color it was reserved for very special and particular uses. He said that the pigment came from a precious rock called *lapis lazuli*. I had never heard those two words in my life.

Then he showed a photo of the rock after it has been pulverized into a thin blue powder. *Poof.* That was me right there. All that I felt was left of me was dust. I tried to hold back my tears and the desire to run up to the altar and sob. He talked about how God was not done with us and that He could turn that dust into a beautiful pigment.

I remembered how the previous summer I had gone to Arizona for a personal retreat with the Lord. On the last day of my trip, as I sat in front of an almost empty lake, I said, "Lord, that's how I feel. The person I used to be is gone, I have dried up. I can see the water mark of where I once was and where I am now, and I am empty. Dry."

As I sat in my rental car, too numb to cry, I felt the Lord speak to my heart very clearly: "*Your satisfaction can only come from me. Not your husband, your children, your career. Your satisfaction must come from me.*"

I wrote a spontaneous song to Him in that holy moment, and for the months that followed I kept singing it constantly, reminding myself of those words. I didn't know how important that warning would be a little over a year later.

Now, I had two visuals of myself: an empty lake and a pulverized rock. Not very cheerful images! Way to go, self-esteem. But I kept seeking the Lord, even as my life continued to change in ways I could not control.

In November of that year, my marriage ended. And all that I had worked on for years was destroyed, along with my heart and hope.

As I drove to my parents house with my two little girls for much needed help, I felt an urgent need to re-read a book called *Hinds Feet on High Places* by Hannah Hurnard. I had read it when I was in college and it had been instrumental for understanding brokenness. I felt the Holy Spirit urging me to read that book.

As soon as I got to my parent's house in Mississippi, I asked them to take me to a bookstore. Providentially, there was only one copy left.

As I read the book, there was a mention of God transforming our sadness into joy and laughter. This was meaningful to me because a few months earlier, God had given me a word through a faith-filled woman who had a dream where the Lord told her, among other things, He would "put laughter on my lips for every tear I had cried."

So, I looked up the verse in my Bible app. It's important to note that I grew up in Puerto Rico, where I spoke Spanish all of my life and read the Bible in Spanish. That day, however, I decided to look up the passage in the English, NIV version. This led me to Isaiah 54, and what I can only describe as a silent sonic boom encounter with the living word of God. I know that sounds strange, but I have no other way to explain it.

I had read this chapter many times in my life, but never like that day, or under these circumstances.

> "For your Maker is your husband—the
> Lord Almighty is his name—the
> Holy One of Israel is your Redeemer; he
> is called the God of all the earth.
> The Lord will call you back as if you
> were a wife deserted and
> distressed in spirit—
> a wife who married young, only
> to be rejected," says your God...Though
> the mountains be shaken and the hills

> be removed, yet my unfailing love
> for you will not be shaken nor my
> covenant of peace be removed," says the Lord,
> who has compassion on you." Is.54: 5-6, 10

I wept as I read, moved by how the Lord was speaking to me in a very intimate and specific way. But when I got to verse 11, I felt like I was in a spaceship from *Star Wars* that went into lightspeed travel in that precise moment.

I felt a force against my chest, a spiritual collision if you will, between my soul and the living word of God. Words that had been spoken through the prophet Isaiah thousands of years ago but that, like a sound wave, were still traveling and touching hearts. And in that room, in that moment ordained in heaven and planned in advance, God met me where I was.

> "Afflicted city, lashed by storms and not
> comforted, I will rebuild you with stones
> of turquoise, your foundations
> with *lapis lazuli*." (italics mine)

I was blown away by how God had carefully moved pieces to get this particular message, on this particular day to me. Had I decided to read my Bible in Spanish, I would have missed it, because that is not the word used in Spanish for that precious rock.

Did my pastor know this was going to happen? Of course not! Did I know this was the Holy Spirit's intention as He moved me towards that book and this passage? Not at all.

But He knew what I needed, and those words kept me going for years. My Maker prepared me for the darkest, most difficult time in my life with beautiful promises I could depend on when I couldn't see my path clearly. Life-altering words that kept me going when I felt like giving up on everything.

And those are just but a few of the ways Jesus has spoken and cared for me in the past years. I could go on and on talking about these things, and I often meditate on them because it is important for me to remember. I am still not fully out of this valley. But His mercy and grace have brought me this far.

Do I have these supernatural God moments every day? No, I don't. But when there is uncertainty, I can look back at these experiences and tell my soul to believe because of what He has done before. Because He is unchanging. Because He is faithful. Because we can trust in Him.

That is the importance of remembering, of writing these things down, of lifting memorials in our homes that remind us of His work in our lives. Because when we lose sight of these things, we also lose sight of our hope and who it comes from: Christ in me, the hope of glory (Col.1:27).

These are the moments that see us through the dark nights. These are the songs that are born from a soul that chooses to honor and worship God in the midst of hardships, even when we don't comprehend what He is planning, or can't hear His voice clearly.

This is the collision of God's grace with your weakness. The miracle that is the God of heaven embracing His children with purpose and sovereignty. The fulfillment of His promise to never leave us or forsake us. The God who keeps His covenant.

Break Through

I need your voice
louder than my thoughts
Your gaze more penetrating
than my doubts
Your comfort more constant
than the pain
Your light brighter than the fury
of this world in darkness

Break through the dense fog
that hides the path on which I should walk
Break through with the strength
with which you established the earth
and split the sea
Ride the heavens to be my aid
and rescue my soul
Break through
Break through, my Lord

Has the Lord spoken to you through a sermon or Bible study recently? What was He speaking to you about? Make your notes here and read these often to remind yourself of what He has said.

Speaker: Date:

Central idea of message:

Speaker: Date:

Central idea of message:

Speaker: Date:

Central idea of message:

Speaker: Date:

Central idea of message:

Speaker: Date:

Central idea of message:

Remember

Consider the Scriptures referenced in these messages during your own devotional time with the Lord. There may be more that He reveals as you go deeper in your study.

Speaker: _______________________ Date: _______________________
Central idea of message: _______________________________________

____

____

____

____

Speaker: _______________________ Date: _______________________
Central idea of message: _______________________________________

____

____

____

____

____

Speaker: _______________________ Date: _______________________
Central idea of message: _______________________________________

____

____

____

____

Speaker: _______________________ Date: _______________________
Central idea of message: _______________________________________

____

____

____

____

Use the following pages to list things that you are thankful for. Our gratitude helps shift the focus from our circumstances to our Savior.

Thank you God for:

Remember

Thank you God for:

Thank you God for:

Thank you God for:

Remember

"*You are my hiding place; you protect me from trouble. You surround me with joyful shouts of deliverance.*" Ps.32:7 CSB

Use the following pages to keep track of your prayer requests. Make sure to update them as the Lord responds, for they will be an encouraging reminder of His power and miracles.

Date:

Request:

Answer:

Date:

Request:

Answer:

Date:

Request:

Answer:

Date:

Request:

Answer:

Date:

Request:

Answer:

Date:

Request:

Answer:

Date:

Request:

Answer:

Date:

Request:

Answer:

"But I trust in you, Lord; I say, "You are my God." The course of my life is in your power..."

Ps.31:14, 15a CSB

Remember

"Be silent before the Lord and wait expectantly for him..." Ps.37:7a CSB

Date:

Request:

Answer:

Date:

Request:

Answer:

Date:

Request:

Answer:

Date:

Request:

Answer:

Date:

Request:

Answer:

Date:
Request:

Answer:

Date:
Request:

Answer:

Date:
Request:

Answer:

Date:
Request:

Answer:

Date:
Request:

Answer:

*Dear Father, I pray for all those who read
and complete these pages. I pray that your
Holy Spirit comforts them in their time of need
and that your light and your truth may guide them
to a deeper intimacy with you. May our hearts learn to
recognize the voice of our Shepherd, so
that we may follow you, even when we
don't understand where you are leading us.*

*May those who ask, receive;
may those who seek, find answers;
and may those who knock find you, the Door.
Keep our hearts and minds rooted in you, and
may our faith be strengthened, even as we wait on you.
May our hearts be full of peace, hope, and
the joy that is only found in you.
In Jesus' name, amen.*

"Let us acknowledge the Lord; let us
press on to acknowledge him.
As surely as the sun rises, he
will appear; he will come to us
like the winter rains, like the
spring rains that water the earth."

Hos. 6:3

Karenlie Riddering is a writer, artist, and speaker born in Puerto Rico. She now calls Georgia home and is the happy mother of two amazing girls and a lover of national parks, Thai food, and traveling. Her other books and productions can be found online. Find her photos @karenliana.

I am thankful for all the people God has used to bless me throughout my life. Some have no idea how they much they ministered to me, while others have stood by me through more than one valley and in times of laughter. Each of my sisters and friends have been instrumental in what I have walked through, and for that, I will be eternally grateful. A special thanks to Marggie Riddering, Janette Cintrón Valentín, Greta Hancock, Debbie McCreary, Rebecca Nealey, and Jonathan Riddering for their help with this journal. These are brave people who love God and inspire others to love Him always.
Thank you.

ISBN: 9798655623309
First Edition

Although the publisher and the author have made every effort to ensure that the information in this book was correct at press time and while this publication is designed to provide accurate information in regard to the subject matter covered, the publisher and the author assume no responsibility for errors, inaccuracies, omissions, or any other inconsistencies herein and hereby disclaim any liability to any party for any loss, damage, or disruption caused by errors or omissions, whether such errors or omissions result from negligence, accident, or any other cause. This publication is meant as a source of valuable information for the reader, and the opinions of the author, however it is not meant as a substitute for direct expert assistance. If such level of assistance is required, the services of a competent professional should be sought.